RAIN AND PEOPLE

NIKKI BUNDEY

 Carolrhoda Books, Inc. / Minneapolis

First American edition published in 2001 by
Carolrhoda Books, Inc.

All the words that appear in **bold** type are explained
in the glossary that starts on page 30.

Photographs courtesy of: Juliet Highet—cover (inset) right / Liba Taylor 7 / Stephen
Pern 12 / Robert Francis 23 / L. Parker 28 / Hutchison Picture Library; Daniel White
13t / Roger Scruton 14b / Impact Photos; Stephen Dalton 5t / Roger Tidman 17t /
Anthony Bannister 29t / NHPA 11t / Philip Sauvain Picture Collection; Bojan Brecelj
—cover (inset) left / DERA 4t / Gil Moti 6 / Mark Edwards 10, 11b, 19t / Boris
Rostami-Rabet 20 / Ray Pfortner 26 / John Maier 27b / Still Pictures—cover
(background), 4b, 15, 16, 25, 29b / The Stock Market; H. Rogers—title page, 22, 24t
/ Dinodia 5b / Eric Smith 8 / S. Grant 13b, 19b / J. Stanley 14t / G. Howe 17b /
Martin Barlow 18 / K. McLaren 21 / Photo Library Int. 24b / A. Tovy 27t / TRIP.

Illustrations by Artistic License/Genny Haines, Tracy Fennell

Carolrhoda Books, Inc.
A division of Lerner Publishing Group
241 First Avenue North
Minneapolis, Minnesota 55401 U.S.A.

Website: www.lernerbooks.com

A ZOË BOOK

Copyright © 2000 by Zoë Books Limited. Originally produced in 2000 by Zoë Books
Limited, Winchester, England

Library of Congress Cataloging-in-Publication Data

Bundey, Nikki, 1948–
    Rain and people / by Nikki Bundey.
        p. cm. — (The science of weather)
    Includes index.
        Summary: Examines how rain affects humans, discussing how it is needed for
drinking water, farming, and the generation of electricity. Includes experiments.
        ISBN 1-57505-494-9 (lib. bdg. : alk. paper)
        1. Rain and rainfall—Juvenile literature. [1. Rain and rainfall.
2. Hydrologic cycle.] I. Title. II. Series: Bundey, Nikki, 1948–
Science of weather.
QC924.7.B84   2001
551.57'7—dc21   99-39664

Printed in Italy by Grafedit SpA
Bound in the United States of America
1 2 3 4 5 6—OS—06 05 04 03 02 01

CONTENTS

WHEN IT RAINS

Splash! Turn up your face and feel the rain. It is cool and wet. It trickles down your neck and drips off your nose. Water is a **liquid**. It can also be a **gas** in the air we breathe. This gas is **water vapor**. It is one of the gases that form a layer, called the **atmosphere**, around our planet.

From space, astronauts can see blue oceans covering large areas of the earth. Bands of white clouds stream around the planet's atmosphere.

Raindrops trickle together to form little streams. A force pulls them downward and into the ground. This force is **gravity**.

Rain makes the earth green, because plants use water for growing. Plants release water vapor into the atmosphere.

As the sun warms lakes, oceans, and rivers, the water **evaporates** into the air. It turns into water vapor. Warm air rises, carrying the vapor. As the air rises, it cools, and the vapor **condenses**, becoming water. Tiny droplets in the air form clouds. Raindrops grow heavy and fall to the ground. The rain drains into rivers, lakes, and oceans. It then evaporates all over again. This endless process is the **water cycle**.

Rain may lie in puddles or soak into the ground. It may run into streams, rivers, lakes, or seas. As water moves, it wears down rocks and shapes the landscape.

A SOURCE OF LIFE

Rain can make us feel cold, wet, and uncomfortable. After a heat wave or dry **weather**, rain is more welcome. Water can cool us down.

Water also keeps us alive. More than half of the human body is made up of water. Blood is mostly salty water. It carries life-giving **oxygen** around the body. Water keeps our **cells** alive.

Girls in Bangladesh collect water from a pump in the street during a rainstorm. Skin is the body's waterproof covering. It contains tiny holes called **pores**. They allow water to pass out of the body, but not into it.

Humans need to drink about two quarts of water each day, but much more in hot, dry conditions.

Water helps our bodies **digest** food. Water cleans us out, too. It carries waste from our bodies in the form of **sweat** and **urine**. We breathe out water vapor.

We have to replace the water we lose from our bodies. About half the water we need comes from our food. We drink the rest. Without rain, there would be no food or drink.

See for Yourself

- How much liquid do you drink each day? Keep a record.
- Before taking a drink, pour it into a measuring cup.
- Make a note of every drink you take, not just water.
- Add up the total for one day and compare the result with that of a friend.

HILLSIDE TO HOME

Streams, rivers, and **freshwater** lakes all provide drinking water. Sometimes we collect and store water in tanks and reservoirs. We cannot drink seawater unless we take the salt out of it. This process, called **desalination**, is expensive.

Rainwater soaks underground. People dig wells to reach it. Sometimes natural **pressure** inside the earth forces the water upward. Sometimes water must be pumped out.

As rainwater seeps down through soil or soft rock, it may be trapped by a layer of hard rock. People must dig through the rock to make a well that can supply freshwater.

Water runs through pipes from springs and reservoirs into towns. We use it for drinking, washing, cooking, and cleaning. Industries such as papermaking use lots of water.

Pipes or channels called **aqueducts** carry water long distances. Gravity and pumps move water through the pipes.

Most water is cleaned before we drink it. Sometimes it is filtered through mesh screens and layers of sand. Chemicals such as **chlorine** kill **bacteria**, or germs, in the water.

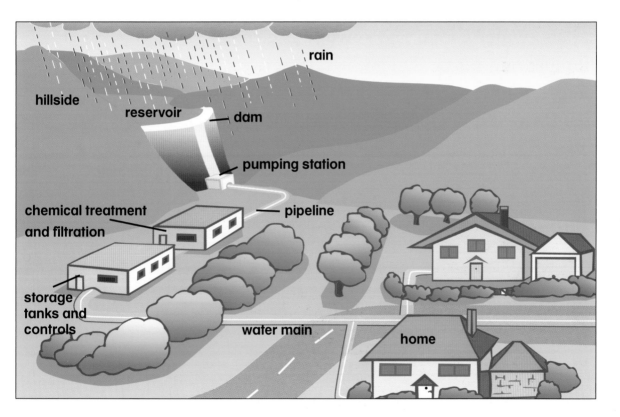

rain

hillside

reservoir — dam

pumping station

chemical treatment and filtration

pipeline

storage tanks and controls

water main

home

See for Yourself

- Wasting water also wastes money.
- Think of ways you can save water at home. Make sure faucets are turned off completely. Don't overfill your bath. Don't leave the water running when you brush your teeth.
- Choose three ways to save water and carry them out each day.

WATER AND HEALTH

Water helps us to keep clean and healthy. We use water to wash our food and our bodies. A rainstorm washes the street, making it clean and fresh.

Water flushes waste from bathtubs, sinks, and toilets. Water containing **sewage** is cleaned in pipes and tanks. Then it is released back into rivers, lakes, and oceans. Wastewater can be reused only if it is properly cleaned.

Safe water supplies are expensive. Not all countries can afford them. Drinking water can easily be poisoned by sewage or chemicals .

Before the 1900s, sewage poisoned many water supplies. Diseases such as cholera were very common. Then people built underground sewers in many cities. Pipes carried sewage away, keeping it from clean water supplies. Cholera still kills many people, especially in poor countries where water supplies are not clean.

Pools where mosquitoes breed are sprayed with chemicals. This spray keeps malaria from spreading.

Standing water can be a health risk for humans. Insects such as mosquitoes breed in ponds. They pass on dangerous illnesses such as malaria and yellow fever. Lakes and rivers may contain a deadly **parasite** that causes the disease schistosomiasis. More than 100 million people suffer from schistosomiasis in Asia, Africa, and South America. For a healthy world, we all need fresh, clean water supplies.

11

RAIN FOR FARMING

Rain keeps plants and animals alive. Farmers fear long periods without rain, called **droughts**.

Cattle and sheep need to drink water. They also need green grass to eat. In very dry lands, herders move with their animals from one **pasture** to another and from one **water hole** to the next. People who travel from place to place are called **nomads**.

Nomads are rounding up sheep in Mongolia. The average rainfall there is only eight inches per year.

Rice first grew in **tropical** river valleys, which often flooded. Rice grows best in wet, muddy conditions. These farmers in Sumatra, Indonesia, are harvesting rice plants.

All crops need water. Rice needs warm, rainy conditions. Other crops, such as millet and sorghum, can grow in areas of low rainfall.

In dry places, pipes and channels carry water to the fields. This system is called irrigation. The water may come from rivers, lakes, or reservoirs. It costs a lot to carry water a great distance. In very dry areas, water may evaporate before reaching the crops.

Sprinklers soak the dry fields around the town of Guadalupe in southern California.

KEEPING DRY

Since **prehistoric** times, people have tried to protect their bodies from rain. They have used animal fur and skins to make warm, dry coats. Some farmers used sheep's wool to make sweaters. Wool contains a grease that keeps out water.

The first raincoat was made in 1832. It was made of cotton soaked in a rubber solution and named a "mackintosh," after the inventor. Modern raincoats are treated with chemicals, oils, and waxes that repel water.

Umbrellas are made from waterproof fabric. Their bell shape shelters us and lets rainwater run off.

To be ready for a storm at sea, sailors wear waterproof clothing from head to foot.

We use **plastics** to keep us dry in a storm. Plastics may be flexible or hard. Some umbrellas are made of plastic, so are some raincoats and boots. Water cannot pass through clothing made of plastic. When rain hits plastic, it runs off and falls to the ground.

Rubber and plastic are used to make waterproof footwear. Thick treads on the soles grip wet, slippery ground. The force of one surface rubbing against another is called **friction**.

ON THE ROAD

Stone, concrete, and **asphalt** make roads strong and protect them from the rain. If roads are not properly drained, rainwater will lie on the surface in puddles. Many roads are built with a **camber**, or slope, so that rainwater flows away into gutters and drains.

Floods and heavy rain have broken up this asphalt road. If roads do not have hard surfaces, the damage can be much worse. Entire highways can be washed away in heavy storms.

Bridges carry people and traffic across rivers and streams. A bridge must be strong enough to stand up against powerful currents and floods after rainstorms.

Rain makes roads slippery. A film of water on a road can make trucks, cars, and bikes start to **hydroplane.** Without friction, tires cannot grip the road. Drivers cannot steer, and cars may skid.

Rain makes it harder for a driver to see clearly. Windshield wipers have rubber blades that push raindrops off the car's window. Why do the blades move more easily over a wet surface than a dry one?

Tires have treads that provide as much gripping power as possible. Tires throw up lots of spray in heavy rain.

BUILDINGS AND RAIN

In dry countries, people sometimes build houses from adobe (dried mud bricks). In wet countries, people use harder materials that will not **dissolve** in the rain. They might use stone, hard-baked brick, wood, concrete, or glass.

In rainy **climates**, roofs are sloped, or pitched. Water easily runs off into gutters and drainpipes. Sometimes people collect the water in tanks or pools for future use.

This pitched roof allows rain to drain to the ground.

These roofs are made of iron sheets. Water can cause metal to rust. Rust eats into metal and creates holes.

Coats of fresh paint protect woodwork from water.

Rainwater can damage buildings. It soaks into bricks and concrete, making them damp and weak. Wet wood can swell, warp, or rot. **Fungus** may grow on damp wood. Rain makes metals such as iron go rusty. All kinds of chemicals, waxes, oils, and coatings can protect building materials from rain and damp.

19

FLOOD CONTROL

Heavy rainstorms cause flooding. The ground becomes **waterlogged** and cannot soak up any more water. Rivers spill over their banks, carrying rocks and boulders along. Over many years, the rocks and water erode, or wear down, the landscape.

Floods can destroy crops and drown sheep and cattle. They can wash away roads and bridges and damage buildings. Floods can also kill people.

Floods in Nicaragua in 1993 destroyed many towns and villages. The floodwater covered the land with mud and sand.

How can we control the power of a flood? Storm drains and ditches allow sudden rains to flow away. **Dams** made of earth or concrete hold back floodwater. High embankments along rivers can keep the water from overflowing.

About 3,700 miles of embankments, called **levees**, line the Mississippi River. They stop the river from flooding farmland.

See for Yourself

- Build a dam across the middle of a plastic bowl or tray.
- Try different materials for the dam—modeling clay, sand, dirt, and stones.
- Fill one side of the bowl with water. Which materials are the most watertight?

WATER POWER

Flowing water can be dangerous, but it can also provide the power to make machines work.

People invented **waterwheels** more than 2,000 years ago. The powerful current of river water moved the wheels around. The wheels carried buckets, which picked up water as they turned. Waterwheels turned millstones, which ground grain into flour. Later waterwheels were used to power machinery in factories.

You can see old waterwheels at this museum in Cornwall, England. Some of these waterwheels were used to power the pumps in tin mines.

Hydroelectric power stations in the Snowy Mountains of Australia make electricity for big cities such as Sydney. The reservoirs also provide water for people and farms.

In modern times, we use water to **generate** electricity. At some reservoirs and lakes, dams hold back great walls of water. Some of the water crashes down through pipes into **hydroelectric** power stations. The rushing water drives huge **turbines**, which make electricity.

See for Yourself

1. Take a sheet of thin cardboard, about four inches by four inches.
2. Fold the cardboard in the four ways seen here.

3. Pinch and push the cardboard into the shape shown.

4. Find a strong drinking straw and make four slits in its end.

5. Put the cardboard into the slits to make turbine blades.

6. Hold the straw loosely in the palm of your hand. Place the turbine blades under a running faucet.

7. How do the blades behave as you change their position against the flow of water? What happens when you turn the water up or down?

RAINFALL SCIENCE

Scientists who study the weather are called **meteorologists**. They measure rainfall in containers called **rain gauges**. They measure the **temperature** of the air—that is, how hot or cold it is. The force of the atmosphere pressing down on the earth is called **air pressure**. Areas of low pressure are often rainy, while areas of high pressure stay dry. The typical weather found in a region is called the climate.

Using rain gauges, scientists monitor rainfall every day at weather stations all over the world.

Satellites in space track the movements of weather systems around the world. The information from satellites helps scientists forecast the weather and understand the earth's climate patterns.

Meteorologists study pictures of the earth taken by satellites in space. These pictures show belts of clouds around the planet. The images help the scientists forecast weather conditions.

Scientists can make rain fall from clouds. Airplanes drop chemicals into clouds, which then **precipitate,** or drop rain or snow. This process is called cloud seeding.

Weather forecasters study satellite images and information from weather stations. Forecasts of rain are important for many different people, from farmers to members of sports teams.

PROBLEM RAIN

Scientists can measure the chemicals in rain and freshwater. Sometimes they find that the water is poisoned, or **polluted**.

Smoke and fumes from factories pollute the air in New York State.

An ancient temple called the Parthenon sits in the heart of the city of Athens in Greece. Pollution has badly damaged the temple. Athens is trying to cut down on air pollution.

Tropical regions, near the equator, receive the most rainfall. Global warming could change weather patterns, bringing less rain to the tropics.

Acid rain forms when chemicals from factories and car exhaust mix with water vapor in the air. Rain that contains chemicals poisons plants, lakes, and wildlife. Acid rain even eats away at the stone of buildings.

Air pollution might be causing **global warming**. Layers of **carbon dioxide** from cars and factories are trapping the earth's heat, making the earth warmer. Rapid climate change may turn some parts of the world into hot deserts, while other parts become stormier and wetter. Governments and scientists are studying ways to reduce air pollution.

A PRECIOUS RESOURCE

A rainy climate is a valuable resource. It provides water for drinking, farming, industry, and hydroelectric power. Many parts of the world are short of rainfall and freshwater. However, water is found in unexpected places, such as underneath the Sahara Desert.

During the rainy season in central Africa, floodwaters flow north along the Nile River. These waters have made the land **fertile**.

People use **shadufs** to raise water from the Nile River. Some of this water is used to irrigate fields.

The San people have lived in the dry lands and deserts of southern Africa for thousands of years. They know how to find water in many hidden places.

People who study water are called **hydrologists**. They look for water by studying photographs taken from airplanes and satellites.

Hydrologists set off explosions that send **shock waves** through the ground. The speed at which the waves travel tells scientists whether the ground has soaked up water or not. Hydrologists drill down to reach the water.

The search for water supplies is more important than ever. Six billion people live on the earth, and we all need to drink clean, fresh water every day.

Space probes are used to explore planets and moons. Scientists are interested in any signs of water, because planets that have water might also have life.

GLOSSARY

acid rain	Rain polluted by chemicals in the air
air pressure	The force with which the atmosphere presses on the ground
aqueduct	A channel or pipe that carries water
asphalt	A black or dark brown substance, made from petroleum
atmosphere	The layer of gases around a planet
bacteria	Tiny organisms, some of which can make us sick
camber	A curved or angled surface
carbon dioxide	A gas, present in the atmosphere
cell	One of the small units making up a living thing
chlorine	A chemical used to clean water
climate	The pattern of weather in one place over a long period
condense	To turn from a gas into a liquid
dam	A barrier preventing the flow of water
desalination	The process of taking salt out of seawater
digest	To absorb food into the body
dissolve	To mix a solid or a gas into a liquid
drought	A long period without rain
evaporate	To change from a liquid into a gas
fertile	Able to produce crops
freshwater	Salt-free water
friction	The force that slows an object as it rubs against another
fungus	Growths such as mold, mushrooms, and mildew
gas	An airy substance that fills any space in which it is contained
generate	To produce something, such as electricity
global warming	A warming of the earth, possibly caused by air pollution
gravity	The force that pulls objects to earth
hydroelectric	Describing power produced by water turbines
hydrologist	A scientist who studies water resources
hydroplane	To skid on a wet road
levee	A high bank that stops a river from flooding
liquid	A fluid substance, such as water

meteorologists	Scientists who study the weather
nomads	People who move around, without a settled home
oxygen	A life-giving gas found in air and water
parasite	A plant or animal that lives on or inside another
pasture	Grass or other plants used for feeding animals
plastics	Materials made from petroleum products
polluted	Poisoned
pores	Tiny openings or holes in the skin
precipitate	To drop rain or snow
prehistoric	The time before written records
pressure	The force with which one thing presses against another
rain gauges	Instruments for measuring rainfall
satellites	Spacecraft that circle a planet
sewage	Water carrying human waste
shaduf	A pole and weight used to raise buckets of water
shock waves	Waves, caused by an explosion, that travel faster than the speed of sound
sweat	Waste water passed from the body through the skin. Sweating cools the body.
temperature	A measurement of heat or cold
tropical	Describing warm, wet regions near the equator
turbines	Wheels with blades turned by gas or liquid
urine	Waste water passed from the body
water cycle	The ongoing process in which rain falls, evaporates, rises, and condenses
water hole	A natural pond where animals come to drink
waterlogged	Soaked and unable to hold any more liquid
water vapor	A gas created when water evaporates
waterwheel	A large wheel turned by moving water
weather	Atmospheric conditions such as heat, cold, rain, sun, snow, clouds, and wind

INDEX

551.57
BUN

Bundey, Nikki.

Rain and people